FRANK LLOYD WRIGHT
THE ROMANTIC SPIRIT

FRANK LLOYD WRIGHT
THE ROMANTIC SPIRIT

CAROL BISHOP

BALCONY PRESS ▪ LOS ANGELES

First Edition

Published in the United States of America
by Balcony Press 2005
Design by David Bishop
Production by Navigator Cross-media
Printed in South Korea

For information address Balcony Press,
512 E. Wilson Suite 213, Glendale, CA 91206

Frank Lloyd Wright: The Romantic Spirit
© Carol Bishop

Library of Congress Card Number: 2004118345
ISBN 1-890449-30-X

Cover/Title page: Hollyhock House, Los Angeles, CA

CONTENTS

INTRODUCTION

Growing up in Chicago I was surrounded by a legacy of impressive architecture, but the houses of Frank Lloyd Wright made an especially deep impression. The essential beauty of his work was evident immediately, yet it was the feelings I experienced while watching his buildings interact with their environments that initiated my interest in his ideas. Wright's romantic philosophy invites us into a dialogue about the way design fuels the spirit of human potential. Coming upon his buildings is like meeting living entities; they speak to us about how architecture encompasses life's desires. You can catch Wright himself whispering through the harmony of his structures. His voice creates a brightness that radiates through anyone who is willing to engage his architecture.

Frank Lloyd Wright defined beauty as the light within the soul of man. This was a parallel to what great architecture could be. By balancing the connections between the parts of a building to the whole, as well as the relationship between the total structure to the adjoining spaces, he conceived an architecture that appealed to the human craving for beauty. Questions about location, how the foundation engages the ground, where the roof meets the sky, the placement of trees and foliage – all of these environmental factors were as significant to him as the structures themselves. His work is evidence that designs from the past can be timeless and inspire subsequent generations to work against a dislocation from nature.

My quest with the work of Frank Lloyd Wright is not only communicating my personal reactions to his designs, but also expanding the discussions inherent in the original work. Through photography I reveal how his architecture can force us to think and feel about the harmony between nature and humanity. This is the Romantic Spirit that originally touched me in the buildings of Frank Lloyd Wright.

– Carol Bishop

FOREWORD

Frank Lloyd Wright's work has been captured in hundreds of publications of drawings and photographs since the elegant Wasmuth Portfolio, Ausgeführte Bauten und Entwürfe von Frank Lloyd Wright, first appeared in 1910. Wright wrote in the introduction to that publication that his drawings were "in no sense attempts to treat the subject pictorially" but rather were "graceful decorative rendering[s] of an idea of an arrangement." Photographs in a complementary volume were much more didactic and realistic in intent. Many artists in the decades since have tried to capture the meaning and magic of his buildings through their particular medium, a few with outstanding success.

Among the recent endeavors, the work of Carol Bishop stands out for its unique approach of combining photography with painting. The resulting images give these twentieth-century architectural icons an aura of near Hawthorne-esque romanticism, imbuing them with a dreamlike quality bordering, in some instances, on ethereal monumentality, which might well serve even the staunchest modern day Wagnerians.

– Margo Stipe
Art Collections Administrator
The Frank Lloyd Wright Archives, Taliesin

PLATES

1 "Fallingwater" Edgar J. Kaufmann Sr. House
Mill Run, Pennsylvania, 1935

2 Charles Ennis House
Los Angeles, California, 1923

3 Frank Lloyd Wright Home & Studio
Oak Park, Illinois, 1889

4 Frederich C. Robie House
Chicago, Illinois, 1906

5 Taliesin III
Spring Green, Wisconsin, 1925-1959

6 Bell Tower, Taliesin West
Scottsdale, Arizona, 1937-59

7 John Storer House
Los Angeles, California, 1923

8 Taliesin Sign, Taliesin West
Scottsdale, Arizona, 1937-1959

9 Riverview Terrace
Spring Green, Wisconsin, 1953

10 Monona Terrace
Madison, Wisconsin, 1997

11 "The Harem" Frank Wright Thomas House
Oak Park, Illinois, 1901

12 Isabel Roberts House
River Forest, Illinois, 1908

13 "La Miniatura" Mrs. George Madison Millard House, Pasadena, California, 1923

14 Isidore Heller House
Chicago, Illinois, 1896

15 Romeo & Juliet Windmill, Taliesin East
Spring Green, Wisconsin, 1896

16 Unity Church
Oak Park, Illinois, 1904

17 Taliesin Fellowship Architecture Studio
Spring Green, Wisconsin, 1925-1959

18 Taliesin III
Spring Green, Wisconsin, 1925-1959

19 Harry C. Goodrich House
Oak Park, Illinois, 1896

20 Thomas H. Gale House
Oak Park, Illinois, 1892

21 George D. Sturges House
Brentwood Heights, California, 1939

22 Midway Barns, Taliesin East
Spring Green, Wisconsin, 1939

23 Unitarian Meeting House
Shorewood Hills, Wisconsin, 1947

24 Scoville Park Fountain
Oak Park, Illinois, 1903

25 Samuel Freeman House
Los Angeles, California, 1923

26 Walkway, Taliesin West
Scottsdale, Arizona, 1937-1959

27 Taliesin Fellowship, Window View
Spring Green, Wisconsin, 1925-1959

28 Walter M. Gale House
Oak Park, Illinois, 1893

29 Herbert Jacobs First House
Madison, Wisconsin, 1936

30 George Blossom House
Chicago, Illinois, 1892

31 Nathan G. Moore House
Oak Park, Illinois, 1895

32 Sunset Terrace, Taliesin West
Scottsdale, Arizona, 1937-59

33 George W. Spencer House
Lake Delavan, Wisconsin, 1902

34 Engineer's Cottage, "'ob 'arth", Taliesin
Spring Green, Wisconsin, 1925-1959

35 Kentuck Knob
Chalk Hill, Pennsylvania, 1954

36 Walter Rudin House
Madison, Wisconsin, 1957

37 Richard Smith House
Jefferson, Wisconsin, 1950

38 Studio, Residence A, Barnsdall
Los Angeles, California, 1920

39 William H. Winslow House
River Forest, Illinois, 1893

40 Annunciation Greek Orthodox Church
Wauwatosa, Wisconsin, 1956

41 Robert P. Parker House
Oak Park, Illinois, 1892

42 Oscar B. Balch House
Oak Park, Illinois, 1911

43 Rollin Furbeck House
Oak Park, Illinois, 1897

44 William E. Martin House
Oak Park, Illinois, 1902

45 Johnson Wax Research Tower
Racine, Wisconsin, 1944

46 Reflecting Pool, Taliesin West
Scottsdale, Arizona, 1937-59

47 "Hollyhock House" Aline Barnsdall Residence
Los Angeles, California, 1917

48 Edward R. Hills House
Oak Park, Illinois, 1906

49 J. Kibben Ingalls House
River Forest, Illinois, 1909

Wyoming Valley Grammar School
Wyoming Valley, Wisconsin, 1956

51 William H. Copeland House
Oak Park, Illinois, 1909

52 Francis Wooley House
Oak Park, Illinois, 1893

53 "Airplane House" E. A. Gilmore Residence
Madison, Wisconsin, 1908

54 Sun Cottage, Taliesin West
Scottsdale, Arizona, 1937-1959

55 Mrs. Thomas H. Gale House
Oak Park, Illinois, 1904

56 Architecture Studio, Taliesin West
Scottsdale, Arizona, 1937-59

57 Fred B. Jones House
Lake Delavan, Wisconsin 1903

58. Charles S. Ross House
Lake Delavan, Wisconsin, 1902

59 Ravine Bluffs Bridge
Glencoe, Illinois, 1915

60 William F. Kier House
Glencoe, Illinois, 1915

61 Peter A. Beachy House
Oak Park, Illinois, 1906

62 W.A. Glasner House
Glencoe, Illinois, 1905

63 Francisco Terrace Apartments Archway
Chicago, Illinois, 1895 (Reconstructed, Oak Park, 1977)

64 Frank Lloyd Wright Home & Studio Addition
Oak Park, Illinois, 1895

THE PHOTOGRAPHER

Carol Bishop is a Los Angeles-based artist and historian originally from Chicago. Her photos and paintings engage the theme of the ways layers of architecture and landscape engage the viewer. She has exhibited extensively in America and Europe, including at the Carousel du Louvre, the Huntington Museum, and Taliesin III and Taliesin West. She is a senior lecturer at Woodbury University.

PLATE LIST

1   "Fallingwater" Edgar J. Kaufmann Sr. House, Mill Run, Pennsylvania, 1935

2   Charles Ennis House, Los Angeles, California, 1923

3   Frank Lloyd Wright Home & Studio, Oak Park, Illinois, 1889

4   Frederich C. Robie House, Chicago, Illinois, 1906

5   Taliesin III, Spring Green, Wisconsin, 1925-1959

6   Bell Tower, Taliesin West, Scottsdale, Arizona, 1937-1959

7   John Storer House, Los Angeles, California, 1923

8   Taliesin Sign, Taliesin West, Scottsdale, Arizona, 1937-1959

9   Riverview Terrace, Spring Green, Wisconsin, 1953

10   Monona Terrace, Madison, Wisconsin, 1997

11   "The Harem" Frank Wright Thomas House, Oak Park, Illinois, 1901

12   Isabel Roberts House, River Forest, Illinois, 1908

13   "La Miniatura" Mrs. George M. Millard House, Pasadena, California, 1923

14   Isidore Heller House, Chicago, Illinois, 1896

15   Romeo & Juliet Windmill, Taliesin East, Spring Green, Wisconsin, 1896

16   Unity Church, Oak Park, Illinois, 1904

17   Fellowship Architecture Studio, Spring Green, Wisconsin, 1925-1959

18   Taliesin III, Spring Green, Wisconsin, 1925-1959

19   Harry C. Goodrich House, Oak Park, Illinois, 1896

20   Thomas H. Gale House, Oak Park, Illinois, 1892

ACKNOWLEDGEMENTS

I am grateful to all the owners of Frank Lloyd Wright's buildings whose appreciation of his architecture has helped preserve the Wright legacy. Thanks also to those who have been so gracious in sharing their time and enthusiasm.

The following people and organizations have made important contributions toward the realization of this project:

Frank Lloyd Wright Preservation Trust
The Frank Lloyd Wright Conservancy
City of Los Angeles Department of Cultural Affairs
Friends of the Hollyhock House
Frank Lloyd Wright Foundation, Taliesin
Frank Lloyd Wright Archives
The Western Pennsylvania Conservancy
Bishop Family
McNellis Family

Special thanks to David, Sharon, Vanessa, Cheryl, and Margo

'Fallingwater' Edgar J. Kaufmann Sr. House, by permission of Western Pennsylvania Conservancy